W9-DIS-241

INDIANS

The First Americans

Pine Road Library
Lower Moreland Township
Huntingdon Valley, Pa.

INDIANS
The First Americans

BY KATHRYN F. ERNST

Illustrations by Richard Smolinski

An Easy-Read Fact Book

Franklin Watts I New York I London I 1979

**To Uncle Dan,
with love**

R.L. 2.4 Spache Revised Formula

All rights reserved
Printed in the United Kingdom
5　4　3　2　1

Library of Congress Cataloging in Publication Data

Ernst, Kathryn F
　Indians.

　(An Easy-read fact book)
　Includes index.
　SUMMARY: Presents the history of American Indians
from 30,000 years ago to the present.
　1. Indians of North America—History—Juvenile
literature.　[1. Indians of North America—
History]　I. Smolinski, Richard.　II. Title.
E77.4.E76　　970′.004′97　　78-13742
ISBN 0-531-02273-0

photograph on page 35
courtesy of the Smithsonian
Institution National
Anthropological Archives,
Bureau of American
Ethnology Collection

The time is 30,000 years ago.

Two great glaciers cover most of Canada and parts of the United States. The ice in some spots is a mile (1.6 km) high.

In other parts of the United States it rains a lot. Trees and grass grow where deserts are today. Winters are warmer. Summers are cooler.

There are beavers as big as grizzly bears. Camels, lions, saber-toothed cats, wolves, small horses, and mammoths live on the Great Plains. Giant mastodons with long reddish hair feed in the forests. But there are no people.

The people who will find America are still in Asia.

These people are hunters. They can make fire.
They wear animal skins. They have knives and
spears made of stone or bone.

But they do not have the weapons to kill a big animal. They can only wound it. Then they follow it until it dies. This means they don't live in one place. They are always on the move.

Time: 28,000 years ago.

For 2,000 years, the hunters from Asia have been moving north as they follow the animals. Now they are on a big land bridge between Asia and Alaska.

They don't know what is on the other side of the bridge. They are just living from day to day.

We can guess that the hunters live in small bands of about 30 people. They have children when they are very young. They often die at an early age.

In the summer they eat birds' eggs and clams. They fish and kill seals. The sun shines almost 24 hours a day.

In the fall they hunt for meat to store for the long, dark, very cold winter. The cold keeps the meat from going bad.

Time: 27,000 to 25,000 years ago.

The hunters have crossed the land bridge. They are now moving down through the Canadian Yukon. We know this because scientists found a caribou bone the hunters used to clean skins.

The bands of people cross the Canadian Rockies. Then they find it! America—the Land of the Big Sky.

Time: 25,000 to 15,000 years ago.

The hunters do well in America. The weather is good. There are plenty of roots, nuts, berries, and animals to eat.

The little bands move all over—from what is now New York to Florida, California, and Texas. Some go as far south as Mexico and Peru.

As time goes by, the bands grow larger—up to 150 people. They add new words to their languages. They make better knives and spears.

With more people, the bands can hunt more safely. They can stampede big animals over cliffs. They can trap them in box canyons. Sometimes they kill much more food than they can use.

Time: 15,000 years ago.

The glaciers in Canada are starting to melt. They had stopped the cold winds blowing down from the Arctic. They had kept America cool in the summer.

Now the ice is melting. Bit by bit for 5,000 years. And the weather in America changes.

Winters are longer and colder.
Summers are hotter. Deserts form
in the West. Less rain falls
on the Great Plains.

Mammoths, mastodons, and
many other big animals die
out. So does the small
American horse.

Time: 10,000 to 5,000 years ago.

Hunting is not as easy as it was. The first Americans spend more time looking for seeds, nuts, and plants to eat.

They learn to make baskets to carry the seeds. They use stones to grind the seeds into flour. They make hooks and nets to catch more fish and small game.

NET MENDER

FISHHOOKS

Instead of following the animals, the first Americans start to plan where they are going. In the Southwest, the people know at what time of year and in what place wild corn is growing and ready to eat. Each year they plan to be there at that time to harvest the corn.

In the East and near the Great Lakes, the first Americans set up camps that they come back to year after year. They make canoes to travel more easily.

This means the bands begin to see each other more often. There is more marrying between bands. There is more trade. More ideas are shared.

Time: 5,000 to 1,000 years ago.

A very important idea in America has come from Mexico. The idea is farming. It takes root in the dry, poor land of the Southwest—where food is always hard to find.

Farming starts with beans and corn. The first corn grown is no bigger than your thumb. It does not have a husk.

The farmers plant many seeds. They build small dams to catch and save water for the plants. The plants grow in groups. The ones on the outside protect the ones inside from birds and desert winds.

The use of farming slowly spreads east and then north. Farming makes life easier. Because of farming, many bands can now live in one place all year round. They become tribes. They can grow food and store it for the winter. They have more time to make beautiful things—baskets, pottery, blankets, and carvings. Some cultures, such as the Hopewellian, become very large and richer than before. They are known as "mound builders."

Time: 1492

By the time Columbus lands his ships, there are around 13 million people in America. (Columbus calls them "Indians" because he thinks he has landed in India.)

In color, some of the first Americans are yellow-white to light brown. Others are a bronze or copper tone. Their eyes are dark. They have straight black hair on their heads. But there is very little hair on the rest of their bodies.

They grow tobacco. Some use copper to make tools and jewelry. Some paint their faces for ceremonies or to show whether they are planning for peace or war.

Altogether, there are around 250 tribes. They have different laws, religions, words, and customs. But many are alike in one important way: The earth is their mother. They do not feel anyone can buy or sell land. Land is for everyone to share.

The people who follow Columbus from Europe do not understand the first Americans—their clothes, customs, or feelings about the land. Many think the Indians are savages. And for the next 400 years, they will fight with the Indians over who owns the land and how it is used.

An Indian prays for rain.

Time: 1600s

The long fight with the Europeans does not begin right away. Indians help the first colonists get started in Jamestown in 1607. They give the Puritans food and show them how to grow corn. But more and more Europeans come. They take more Indian land for their farms and houses.

The first Indian chief to fight for the land is called King Phillip. At first he and his people win battles. But on August 12, 1676, King Phillip is killed. His wife and son are sold as slaves.

King Phillip

Time: 1862

From King Phillip's time through the mid 1800s white people keep coming to America from Europe.

They live in cities. They make farms out of the forest land. Some get along well with the Indians. But many do not. There is fighting during all of this time.

Then the Homestead Act is passed in 1862. This means anyone over 21 can get 160 acres (64 hectares) of land—just by living on it and working it.

White families go West to find land. They often do not understand that they are taking Indian hunting grounds. Indians attack their wagons. The Army moves West to protect the settlers.

Time: 1869

The first railroad to go across the country is finished. The trains frighten the buffalo. They bring more settlers. Indians tear up the tracks. They attack the trains. But they can't stop the settlers.

By 1885, millions of buffalo have been killed by white men for their skins. The bones are worth money too. They can be made into fertilizer and china. The Indians can't count on buffalo for food anymore. There aren't enough of them left.

Time: 1900s

It is over 400 years since
Columbus landed.

Many Indians have been killed.
Some have been killed by guns. Others
are dead from European diseases or
hunger. Still others have been killed by long,
forced marches.

Now most of the first Americans are on
reservations. They get their food from the
government. There are not enough jobs.

An old Yuma woman says, "In the old times we
were strong. We used to hunt and fish. We raised our
little crop of corn . . . . Now all is changed. We eat the
white man's food and it makes us soft. We wear the
white man's heavy clothing and it makes us
weak . . . . When you come, we die."

Time: 1911

A hungry man is found. His hair is burned to show he is sad. He is the last Yahi Indian in California. He has been hiding from white people for 40 years. Now they have found him.

He tells white teachers about Yahi tools, medicines, laws. It hurts him to talk about his family. They are all dead.

In 1916, he also dies, from tuberculosis.

Time: 1924

A law is passed making the first Americans citizens of the United States. They can vote. They also have to pay taxes.

Time: World War II

Many Indians fight in the war. Indian languages are used to send secret messages. Indians are scouts behind enemy lines. Many receive medals for bravery.

Time: 1950s

More Indians move off reservations. They are looking for jobs. The Mohawk Indians are known as great steelworkers. An Indian woman, Maria Tallchief, is one of the world's greatest ballet dancers.

Time: 1960s

The United States starts paying more attention to Indians. Indians sue the government for lost land and broken treaties. President Lyndon Johnson says Indians must have the same rights and chances as everyone else. "The first among us must not be last."

Time: 1970s

Life on reservations is beginning to get better. There are more schools and better hospitals. Indians are starting more businesses. Some choose to live by their old customs. Some do not. But all of America has become more aware of the first Americans. Their history. Their customs. And the way life used to be before the Europeans came.

INDEX